WOMAN UP :

The Ultimate Guide

to Embracing Your

Superpower

by

Shackysha Renée

6 Ways to Woman Up: A Guide to Help
Women Tap Into their Superpower

Printed in the United States of America

ISBN 9781705633540

www.womanupenterprise.com

Dedication

To the women in my family...

I see you. I admire you. I love you.

You are appreciated and the world is

better because of your love, strength, and

resilience.

Preface

Growing up in a huge Caribbean family, women are the pillars. I am surrounded by all different types of women: single, married, separated, wealthy, poor. The list goes on! Although each woman differs in marital and socioeconomic status, the common denominator is their constant yearning for purpose and identity. They are all trying to become the best version of themselves while trying to climb the corporate ladder, start their own business and or raise a family. I have always been in awe of their resilience and tenacity. I remember thinking, "Wow, these are some bad Mama Jamas! If only..."

As I became older, I began to observe and study a woman's body language and discern her energy. I knew in an instant if a woman cried in the bathroom before returning to her desk, if a woman was overwhelmed but was trying to push through by smiling, if a woman was sick and tired of being sick and tired. Yet, the woman still showed up and showed out. The women I encountered showed up *despite* their mental and or physical chaos, and still completed the task at hand. Those women became me.

My passion for mentoring was sparked when I went to college, Hampton University. As a Resident Assistant, I saw a lack of confidence and uncertainty in the girls that I mentored. It was almost as if these ladies were unaware of how powerful they were and the value they possessed. I witnessed women limiting themselves to more traditional roles when choosing a major or future profession. I witnessed women settling for whatever was given to them, financially, physically, spiritually or mentally. I witnessed women modifying their dreams to accommodate the emotions and egos of simple-minded individuals. As a result, I taught my girls how to hone in on their superpower through a mentorship series. This series primarily focused on assisting college freshmen on how to identify areas of improvement. I developed tailored approaches for each individual for said goals; whether academically, professionally or personally.

*   *   *   *   *

It is my intent that every woman who reads this book gains additional insight to who they are and walks into their purpose. I want women to embrace their complexities, feel empowered, and most importantly take time to take care of themselves!

Table of Contents

1

OWN YOUR SUPERPOWER, GIRL !

Superpower [so‾opər‚pou(ə)r/]

Noun: power greater in scope or magnitude than that which is considered natural or has previously existed.

I t's a girl!", the doctor said. Just like that, the butterflies began to fly, the birds began to chirp and the heavens opened up on Earth. What a time to be alive, isn't it? Too theatrical? Take 2.

Sweet baby Jesus said, "Big homie Adam, you cannot do this thing called life by yourself. I am going to create a helpmate, just for you."

So God made it do what it do and voilà, Woman was created. Too religious? Let's try this one more time...

Woman. A flower that blooms without nutrients. She bends, but does not break.

Being born a woman is both an honor and privilege. Being a woman is a superpower that everyone wants the benefit of, but no one wants the responsibility. To be quite honest, not everyone can handle the responsibility. You are chosen.

A superpower is defined as a power greater in scope or magnitude than that which is considered natural or has previously existed. In other words, we are abnormal creatures that exude greatness!

As a woman, we have the innate capability to nurture and love unconditionally. We have the innate capability to multiply anything that is given to us, whether it may be monetarily, spiritually, or physically. We have vision, wisdom and tenacity to make anything come to fruition. We have the innate capability to discern someone's intention from galaxies away. We have the innate capability to teach and heal a nation. Now can you imagine if all women were to be respected by other women and the rest of society? What a sight that will be.

*   *   *   *   *

Women have been the driving force for radical change in various communities for centuries; whether their contribution came from physically being at the forefront of all causes such as pro-choice, voting, or demanding equal pay. Women have been the voice of reason behind every great male leader. They are the primary person that takes on domestic duties to ensure their spouse can be the dominating force they are known to be. Let me put you on to some *fierce* women that have used their superpower to evoke radical change.

Women are the shit! From Sojourner Truth in the 1850's, *Ain't I a Woman?* to Susan B. Anthony who began actively fighting for women's voting rights in 1870. From Gloria Steinem to Bella Abzug and

Betty Friedan who established a caucus that aided women to find their voice in government. From Sally Ride flying to the moon in the 1980's to Halle Berry becoming the first African- American woman to win an Oscar for best actress. And to the beloved Michelle Obama for being the first Black First Lady of the United States of America!

Now that you are aware that you come from greatness, here are a few phrases that you can keep in your back pocket to help remind you of your superpower.

1 *"It's a girl!"* This is one of the most valuable expressions that is often used to let the world know that you have arrived! It is a statement that most people tend to disregard or deem as invaluable because "we all can be great human beings".....yeah but no. Having the privilege to be chosen as the vessel that brings life into this world, the ability to multitask and prophecy over things, is one that only a woman is born with.

2 In the words of J. Cole, *"Pussy is power. That proud feeling we get knowing that pussy is ours."*

Listen, by no way am I encouraging women to use their gold mine to manipulate any person or any situation. But baby girl, please understand that *you* call the shots.

You set the standards and demand the respect that you desire. *You* create the aura you want attract. Men will do anything, and I mean ANYTHING, just for the idea of being in your presence. Just from the thought of you being their 'only one'.....all motivated by your gold mine, that *thang* between your thighs.

Remember, *that thang* is yours and *you* decide who you want to share it with.

8

You decide when and where you want to use that thang. It is not controlled by any male or female nor does it *belong* to any man, person or child. You hear me? That *thang* is yours and yours only!

3 "He who finds a wife, findeth a good thing. And obtains favor from the Lord." This is

scripture from the good book, Proverbs 18:22. Hallelu!

For those of you who have downloaded the Power Pack, then you have heard me say this... Sis, you are a vibe! Understand the value and aura you bring to any setting.

9

Although the scripture mentions wife, let's be honest, you have to court before you date and date before you marry. But the strength of a woman is in her ability to enhance and multiply anything that sets foot in her vicinity. When in a relationship, a woman leverages her intuition to prevent and redirect. She takes dreams and bring them to fruition. A woman powerfully encourages you to be better, but gently loves you through your pain.

It is clearly noted in the bible, a man will not reach his fullest potential or access all that God has to offer him *until* he finds you. But until then, continue to work on yourself in all aspects: spiritually, physically, mentally, and emotionally.

*   *   *   *   *

Similar to any superhero, one must know how to use their superpower so that it can be used at the right time to ensure maximum impact.

Throughout this book, I will provide tools and scenarios that will teach you how to hone into your superpower and become a better you, unapologetically! It is my intent that each of you will understand the value you possess and remind you to never let anyone interrupt your life long journey

to becoming a better you.

2

#KnowYourMinistry

Now we finna take y'all to church.....know your ministry. For those of you who may not be familiar with the church structure, a ministry is an activity that is carried out by members of a church. Some examples of this activity can be singing, dancing, mentoring, community outreach, finance, and many more. The options are endless! People join a ministry because of common belief in the goal of the ministry.

Note: Not everyone participating in ministry is good at it, but they certainly have a passion for it.

*   *   *   *   *

I am known for saying 'Know your ministry' amongst my family and friends. "Kysha, you should just go on a few dates!" *Nah, that's not my ministry.* "Kysha, you should socialize a bit more." I. Don't. Like. People...that's *not my ministry.* "Kysha,

14

you need to learn how to fold your clothes properly!" Umm...as long as everything fits in the bag...*It. Ain't. My. Ministry.*

In all seriousness, knowing your ministry is acknowledging your strengths, addressing and improving upon your weaknesses, and most importantly getting to know yourself inside and out. What makes you tick, what/who are your triggers? What are your passions? Do you see where I am going with this? Knowing your ministry is the primary step to Woman Up. It is essential because this superpower will align you to your purpose and allow you to walk into your destiny.

Please understand that the journey to self- discovery will be one of the hardest things you will have to do in this lifetime. Knowing your ministry (aka you), is an iterative process and a life-time commitment. You will have moments of defeat, periods of depression and or frustration, times where you just want to give up because it is just that much easier to care for and 'fix' others. Hence why most women tend to think every person is a damn project, but I digress.

This is the most important superpower you have and you must protect it at all cost! Protect your mind. Protect your peace. Protect you. This is the key to fulfilling your passion and aligning to your destiny. Know yourself. #Knowyourministry.

We often see movies such as *Eat. Pray. Love.* where an individual is on a quest to "find themselves." They travel across the world and start their spiritual journey. Then Aha! The magic happens. They have "found themselves." I am here to tell you, do not 'find yourself.' *Address* yourself. Address yourself and all the ugly truths.

Address yourself and mend the poor habits that were taught to you your entire life. Address yourself and mend the learned behavior that you have developed as a defense tactic for survival in this cruel world. Address yourself on the basis that no one should ever know you more than you know yourself.

Fact: Knowing your ministry is easier said than done. I know because I have had to do it; I am still doing it. I have suffered from depression. I have had moments when I felt alone, defeated, and overlooked despite having many people around me.

Let me repeat...this will be one of the hardest journeys that you will ever encounter in life because you have to address the monsters that have shaped your outlook on life. You have to look in the mirror and not only acknowledge your current physical, emotional, mental, and spiritual state, but you have to find healthy ways to improve them.

No you cannot say, "Well that's just the way I am" or , "I've been this way my entire life." Address your issues as soon as possible because hurt people, hurt people. Misinformed people, misinform people.

19

Unaware people evoke entitlement. And entitlement breeds ignorance. You can be one of the nicest people in the entire world, but if you have an 'ugly' side (which everyone does) that you have yet to address, you can feed a monster that can do more harm than good.

So how do you get to #KnowYourMinistry? Well I am glad you asked...

1. Take consistent me time

2. Become comfortable being in your own presence

3. Leverage your surroundings to build discernment

4. Trust your intuition

*   *   *   *   *

1 By nature, women are the fixers. We take on everyone's burdens and emotions while trying to 'do us'. While 'doing us', we never take a moment to assess our mental, physical, emotional and spiritual state.

Taking consistent me time is essential to the #knowyourministry movement. Me time is setting time aside to do things that make you feel good, also known as internal validation. Take time for you and enjoy it. Revel in it. Did you hear what I said ladies? E N J O Y I T.

Some examples of *me time* are:

- Having a Girl's Night

- Traveling

- Listening to music and singing *very* loudly (creating new lyrics of course)

- Meditating

- Sitting and doing absolutely **NOTHING** (I know I gave some of y'all a heart attack)... but seriously do nothing!

2 As you begin to seek the things that satisfy your internal validation, I want you to try doing some of these things alone. Travel—alone. Turn on your favorite song, dress up and shake what ya mama gave ya—alone. Be the vibe that you want to attract!

I am the master of alone time. Not even my own mother is invited to my *me time* sessions. That is how much I value my own company....and I am quite comfortable with it too! My friends try to plan events that require me to share my space with others; quite frankly, if I am not ready to share my space with you, you simply cannot enter. I enjoy my own company so much that I try to figure out ways to one day be married and live in separate homes! I know, crazy. That's why I am still going to therapy... we are still *addressing* that.

The concept of going on public dates with yourself can be awkward at first, just like any other first date. Similar to any new encounter, lower your expectations but never your standards. Lower your expectations of what you think a solo date should be and just let it be. What is the worst that can happen? Someone thinks you are lonely? Weird? Well, that sounds like a personal problem. Let them take *their* concerns about *your* business to the Lord in prayer.

As you become more acquainted with yourself, you will see how much easier it will become. Some tips on how to become comfortable with your own presence are below!

Travel? Plan a trip with some close friends. Arrive at your destination a day or two earlier. Book an excursion, have a spa day, sit by the pool and become best friends with the bartender!

Movies? Do a matinee because there tends to be more 'seasoned' folk in the crowd and sometimes you may even have the entire theatre to yourself! Buy your snacks from the supermarket, bring a big comfy sweater, and laugh/cry for the duration of the movie. Remember... there is no one in there.

Dinner? Catch up on your favorite *Netflix* series, watch *YouTube* videos, scroll through *Instagram*, read a book and order food. The choice is yours. By using a medium such as an iPad or a book, you can avoid the awkwardness of trying to figure out where you should look and what you should do with your hands. Trust me, I have been there before!

When you begin to enjoy your presence, you can filter out unwanted energies and most importantly, protect your peace. Trust me, enjoying your own company will save you many disappointments and rescheduled outings with family and friends that will never happen.

There will be change in relationship dynamic. Priorities will change for you and your friends; people will get married and have kids, or go to school. So it is key for you to understand that doing things by yourself is most beneficial because you will be waiting a thousand lifetimes for everyone to be available to do something with you. And that is a fact!

*　　*　　*　　*　　*

Knowing your ministry is identifying your strengths, acknowledging and improving on your weaknesses. In other words, we know that everyone walks around with baggage. They bring baggage to relationships: platonic, business, and romantic. When you #knowyourministry and I mean you *know* the smallest thing that makes you tick, what makes your heart smile and how to enjoy your presence, you will at a minimum, be able to identify the items in your luggage. You will be able to say, "Hey, I have childhood trauma that has caused me to act like_____. To deal with this childhood trauma I have to _____. I have learned that this tactic works/does not work." Do you see where I am going with this? Every person has their flaws, but it is up to you to acknowledge your flaws and improve on them. Do not make excuses!

3 Leverage your surroundings to build discernment. Discernment is the ability to judge well. As women, we are more observant of body language and energies more than we are of verbal communication. Our emotional radars become more sensitive whenever we enter a room. We know when something is off. We may not know what *it* is at the moment, but we just know. Sounds crazy, huh? But WE ARE ALWAYS RIGHT THOUGH. I digress.

Here is what I want you to do the next time you are in a group setting. Allow

31

yourself to feel the energy of those around you. Observe their body language and mannerisms. Is the energy good, slightly off, neutral? Now listen up ladies, I know sometimes (most times), we can get in our own head and start creating scenarios that have yet to occur, probably *will* never occur and we go crazy! I said all that to say this: Not everyone you encounter is going to give you a "feeling." There will be some energies that are neutral. They are not bad; they are not good...they're simply just there. The key takeaway is to feel the energies that make you feel some type a way, good or bad. As you begin to experience this feeling (whatever that may be), start to ask yourself the following questions (internally of course):

Have you felt this feeling/energy before? If so, what happened when you felt this feeling? Take a mental note of what is going on. What are people doing, saying, wearing. Did anyone's body language change? Facial expression? Can you think of possible (logical) scenarios that can happen (if you haven't done so immediately after acknowledging something is wrong) in this situation?

SB: Sis, did I mention to *try* to maintain composure on your face. Do not elude that all of these thoughts are running through your head....because you just may look scary AF. Remember, the key to owning your superpower is learning how to control it.

After time has passed a few minutes, hours or sometimes days, *did anything happen? Was it anything that you thought would have happened? What changed?* Remember how you felt, what you felt and what the results were.

As your discernment begins to strengthen, you can leverage your discernment for interviews, helping family and friends prevent major pitfalls and disappointments, or future business ventures. If something does not feel right, don't do it! Read that again. I did not say if something is uncomfortable do not do it. If you feel an energy that disrupts your spirit, simply #chuckupthedeuces and try again next time!

4 Trust your intuition. Luckily for us, we are born with intuition. According to Merriam Webster dictionary,

intuition is a thing that one knows or considers likely from instinctive feeling rather than conscious reasoning. You know that 'voice' that tells you homeboy ain't it, but you *luh* him? Then boom, six months later you break up and claim that you "saw the signs." You know good and damn well your INTUITION told you something was up seven eleven times, but you chose to ignore it.

Discernment feeds intuition. Discernment will allow you to quickly assess your surroundings to determine if there is a siiitttttuuuuuaaaatttiiiiiooonnn,

36

while your intuition will tell you to get the hell out, and sat down. Your intuition will tell you what is *really* up...time and time again. Trust it.

The sole purpose of the #knowingyourministry is knowing your strengths and weaknesses and being so in tuned with who you are, your likes and dislikes. Now go be prosperous and get in to it!

3

KNOW YOUR

WORTH &
REMEMBER YOUR
VALUE

We are women! We are worthy and highly valuable, regardless of what society does or say to minimize our contributions. Unfortunately, we are conditioned to have the Superwoman Complex. We think that we have to be everything for everyone at all times. "I am woman. Hear me roar!" I am here to tell you, "that's a naw from me, dawg!" Within this chapter, I am going to share key rules to help remind you of your worth and value.

Knowing your worth comes from #knowingyourministry. You understand the value and strength that you bring to *any* setting because you have taken the necessary steps to build your discernment and trust your intuition. Let's get into it!

*   *   *   *   *

Rule No. 1: Never allow anyone to treat you less than how you treat yourself. If you are wondering what that looks like for *you*, then please revisit the last two chapters. We often hear "Don't let anyone treat you less than you deserve." But let's

40

call a spade a spade. We know *what* we deserve. We know *how* we should be treated. Yet we still allow employers, spouses, children, family members, friends and society to take advantage of us. Use yourself as a baseline as to how everyone should treat you. Like I said in the Power Pack, and in chapter two...Be the vibe you want to attract!

P.S. If you have not subscribed to our newsletter, do so now so you can get your FREE version of the Power Pack today! Visit www.womanupenterprise.com

Rule No. 2: Put yourself in your favorite love song. Yes, I said it! You know that jam that you play when you're all up in your feelings. The song that has you thinking about walking down the aisle, starting a family, growing old together with that one special person for the rest of your life...even though homeboy does not even know *y'all* in a relationship? Yeah, that song!

Replace all the pronouns of your favorite love song with your name and envision yourself when the song is directed towards bae, boo, bestie, baby...whatever

42

the hell you call that special person. If you do not feel that same feeling for yourself when you make that switch, go read chapter 2...again!

Here is an example. One my favorite "in my feelings" song is *Beautiful Surprise* by India Arie. The whole song is a vibe. But listen here, the second verse just touches the hort (heart) and *all* the depths of my soul!

You are everything I asked for in my

prayers

So I know my angels brought you to

my life

43

Your energy is healing to my soul

You are a beautiful surprise

You are inspiration to my life

You are the reason why I smile...

Now baaaaaby...if I feel this way about someone else and do not feel that way about myself, IT IS A PROBLEM! Why? Because you will continue to find yourself in situations that are unfulfilling.

I want *my prayers* to become a reality. I want to be grateful that *I am* the person that I have been praying for. I want *my energy*, vibe and aura to heal *my* soul. I am

44

my inspiration. *I am* the reason *I* smile. *I am* my most beautiful surprise because I am constantly changing and healing for the better. Catch my drift sis? Good.

Let's be real, that *thing* that you are searching for when you are not self- aware will have a major impact on your journey to self- discovery. It has the potential to be a distraction. The combination of power and influence is a lethal weapon. So it is critical that you take the necessary steps to love and address every dimension of you to ensure no one or anything can have power and influence over you. Everything that you expect out of a healthy relationship, be sure to be that for yourself first.

Rule No. 3: Understand what type of vibe you bring to an environment and own it. For example, although I walk around with what some may call 'The Resting Bitch Face', people from work have always said that I always have a smile on my face and I am fun to be around. The same thing with family and friends...besides the fact that I am in the ministry of bartending and ALWAYS being the hostess with the mostest, I bring good vibes.

46

On the contrary, my honesty and the way in which I may say things can be too direct for some people to accept or flat out rude. This can kill a vibe and have everyone in their feelings...and not in a good way.

A major component of the Woman Up movement is to be self- aware; own your shit whether it is good or bad. Observe how people act when you are around. Do you kill the vibe? Do people instantly get quiet? Are people excited when you are around. Again, observe the energy. If you bring an unpleasant vibe, figure out why and find ways to improve on it.

47

*　　*　　*　　*　　*

So now that I have provided you with the key rules to help you understand your worth, let's move on to remembering your value. What good is knowing your worth if you do not value it?

Often times, we tend to undermine our value and forget we have this God given superpower; we are WOMAN. We may discredit our superpower because we did not check everything off of our To-do list. We may *forget* because people at our jobs undermine our intelligence constantly. Sis, you got the juice. What did the doctor say? "IT'S. A. GIRL!" What did the media say? "PUSSY. IS. POWER?" What did Yoncé say? "WHO RUN THE WORLD? GIRLS" Need I say more. Once Yoncé said it, it must be true...duh?!?!

Let's talk about some tips for remembering your value!

*   *   *   *   *

Tip No. 1: Time is of the essence. Value and time often go hand in hand. With that being said, understand that time is the most expensive, inexpensive thing that you possess. Expensive, because once time is gone you cannot get it back. Regardless of socioeconomic status, religion, race, you will not be able to get time back. I guess that is why people charge so much for it. Inexpensive, because it does not require monetary value to give your time and energy to a person or a cause.

Tip No. 2: Remember your why. Remember why you embarked on this journey. Remember all the sleepless nights, moments of frustration and the uncomfortable situations that you had to overcome to become the person you are

50

now. Whether you are at your final destination or not, remember, you

are the prize, ALWAYS!

Tip No. 3: Get you a power pose. Not proper English, I know. But I said what I said! According to Forbes, a power pose is an expansive, confident body posture that makes us feel confident. How do you find your power pose, you ask? Simple. "Pose for the camera now. *Flick. Flick. Flick.*" Turn on your favorite song and get to dancing, singing and striking poses in the mirror... and POSE multiple times. Embrace the feeling. Find your angles. Do you feel sexy? Empowered? Not so much...that's fine! This will take some time. Remember, OWN YOUR SUPERPOWER! You do not like your arms, that's fine. Turn your power pose session into a try on haul, a runway, a fashion show. Now you can kill two birds with one stone. Find an outfit that makes you look POPPINGTON, dress your insecurities, and find your angels for the gram. I would call that a win- win!

But seriously....Always start with Yoncé. Sis will have you saying to any and everybody, "I just might get your song played on the radio station", but you don't even know anyone at a radio station. Or she will have you singing, "I might take him on a flight on my chopper!" but you are scared of heights and still whippin' your hooptie around! Moral of the story: Yoncé makes EVERYONE feel better, so ride out and GET YOU A POSE!

Tip No. 4: Reflect on three women you admire; it can be a celebrity or family member (past or present) or a colleague. This rule has kept me both grounded and motivated to keep following my dreams. During moments of frustration and defeat,

I would envision my top three women and reflect on the adversities that they have endured, understand their impact to society, family dynamic, and the professional realm.

Just to know that my role models are *still* here. *Still* impacting. *Still* influencing and making their mark in the world is enough motivation for me. My top three women are obviously my mama, Oprah, and Sarah Jakes Roberts.

I guarantee any woman that you look up to, family member or celebrity, has a story of resilience, ambition and determination. The more 'successful' they appear to be, the deeper the story.

Fun fact: You have a story to tell too, baby girl! So keep pushing. e the person you want your daughter to look up to.

When in doubt, use the aforementioned rules to remind yourself of your worth and value.

4

ACKNOWLEDGE
YOUR
ACCOMPLISHMENTS

When attempting to explain the strength of a woman, the question of "Can you have it all?" or "How do you juggle it all?" typically comes up in conversation. Although primarily targeted at moms, it is a question that is asked entirely too often of women than it is of men. It is a question that society has dropped in the female space and left it there for us to compete with one another, constantly placing additional stressors to be 'perfect'. Similar to any minority community, the primary goal is to create an environment of separation via psychological programming.

Women are more likely to be asked, "how do you juggle it all?" as if to 1) subtly acknowledge that men and women's responsibilities are not equal in scope or 2) to discreetly be in awe of how much a woman can juggle and still look bomb AF while doing it! When that question is asked, that is society's way of saying, "Hey, I see you girl. You doing the damn thing! I don't know how you do it, but I am in awe of what you do because I could NEVER...." Needless to say, men know you are powerful. Children know you are powerful. Hell, women know you are powerful. So the question is why don't you?

I would not be a Leadership and Lifestyle Coach if I did not give it to you straight, no chaser. Can women have it all? Yes, but not at the same time. No one can have it all at the same time. No chic nor child, male or female. I know your blood pressure is probably boiling, but hey #suchislife. Let's break this down.

At any given moment in your life you can have your list of goals; some checked off, some a work in progress, some not yet started. Your list of goals can be:

- I want to be married by 28
- Have 4 kids by 35

59

- Purchase a home by 30

- Get a graduate degree

- Become manager, partner, CEO of a company by 35

Did you get married and give birth at the same time? Did you become CEO and purchase your home at the same time? From the list above, there is no way in hell! Now on the contrary, you can easily acknowledge what you have acquired at that given point in time.

Reality is that you cannot push out a baby, sign the deed to your house and become partner of your company the SAME DAMN TIME. Logically there is a sequence to the aforementioned events.

It is ok to not have things figured out and accomplished by these crazy ass deadlines. These deadlines are either ones that we created for ourselves or society has force fed to us. You are in a lane of your own. Look at where you have started and what you have accomplished. Be proud that you came, you saw, and FUCKED SHIT UP! You could have fucked shit up in the worse way, but the silver lining is that it becomes a lesson learned. It provides you

61

with perspective and helps with redirection. Pat yourself on the back!

On the other hand, you could have FUCKED SHIT UP in the best way and just nailed that presentation, that interview, that hectic day. Just let go of societal standards, your Superwoman Complex, and do you boo! Move at your own pace. Acknowledge who you are and all that you bring to the table. Hell, I am 1000% sure you built the table, you stained it and varnished it, and served up a feast.

So what you made a to- do list for the day and everything did not get checked off?

62

That's ok—you managed to get *something* done (whether it was on your to-do list or not). You got home and you did not feel like cooking so you gave the kids PB&J.....that's ok. They did not go to bed hungry and now they will appreciate the days when you are trying to give them *real* food!

Pat yourself on the back. Be your own cheerleader because not everyone is going to cheer you on. Remember, you are the prize. You are a vibe. You are that chick! Own that superpower, hunty!

5

TREAT YOURSELF

...WITHIN THE MEANS OF YOUR OBLIGATIONS

Treat yourself is a phrase that is often used to describe the action of one spending their hard earned money on themselves; another way to justify silly or unnecessary purchases for immediate satisfaction.

As women it is our primary instinct to nurture, often worrying about everyone else's well-being. This can be a two-edged sword because although a woman's instinct and nurturing spirit can discern when someone needs help, she ends up damaging herself because it takes time away from her self- care.

Women tend to be everything for everyone and very few people can actually be *that* thing that we need. In an article by *USA Today*, women are 66% more likely to exert more brain power when taking time for themselves (i.e., vacations, going for a pedicure). Girl, you are doing too much! Sit down and treat yourself.....within the means of your obligations. Kysh, what the hell does that mean? Treat yourself based on how much time you have, how much money you have relative to your short term and long term on your goals.

I understand that life happens, but we regroup and keep it trucking. You may have made a mistake, or two or three. You may have gone to the "wrong" school or majored in a subject that you really have no interest in. Or you may have had an unplanned

66

pregnancy and now the baby is here—alive and in charge, running your life that *you* thought you had control of. You finished school and now you are trying to repay student loans and move out your parents' house. I get it, I get it. All of it!

As previously stated, we can go from one extreme to the next when it comes to treating ourselves. Sometimes we can be on the lower end of the spectrum where you cannot even fathom the idea of treating yourself because you *"have to"* help mom and dad with your siblings. You cannot treat yourself because who is going to watch the baby? Or on the flip side, I deserve this because the grass is green and the sky is blue. Now you are   left complaining about how you should have prioritized what needed to be prioritized (*rolls eyes). This is why I say treat yourself within the means of your obligations.

Treating yourself within the means of your obligations will eliminate FOMO (fear of missing out), keep you on track with your life goals and most importantly, not give you the chance to become complacent and disregard your responsibilities. Before

I provide some tips, I want to share this story.

* * * * *

One Christmas, I gave my parents a handwritten letter which basically said, "Do you, boo"! We (the kids) are grown. If you want to relocate to another state and or find a new job outside of the state we live in, go ahead. You want to travel to see family in another state?—go ahead. Neither of them were asking for permission, but we gave our consent anyways. *Both* of my parents read the letter and received the message. However, they both had different interpretations.

My dad took the first pass of 'treat yourself', but not within the means of his obligations. He purchased his ticket to Florida to visit his siblings, packed his bag, and did not tell ANYONE that he was going anywhere until the morning of because well... he needed a ride to the airport. You may ask what's wrong with him going to Florida when I encouraged him to spread his wings? The *"within the means of your obligations"* part. Let me set the scene: our family of **six** had one car to share amongst each other during this specific time.

End scene.

Now you can only imagine how this situation goes left very quickly. The only way to make this work and the only way we *have been* able to make this work was **constant** communication.

My mom was a Correctional Officer at the time and it was her weekend to work. She typically worked 16-hour shifts. My youngest brother had basketball practice in another state, and another brother had to get to work. Just in case you were wondering, I have three (younger) brothers. Anyways, because my dad wanted to treat himself, not within the means of his obligations, my mom had to figure it out. She had to figure out how she would get to work on time after dropping my dad at the airport and get my brother to practice. Thankfully, my mom has ALWAYS prioritized her children over her work. Needless to say, she figured it out. Everyone got to where they needed to be on time...except for her. My dad's lack of communication and prioritization created unnecessary chaos for that weekend.

*   *   *   *   *

On the other hand, my mom, after almost twenty years of working in Pennsylvania to raise us, decided to start looking for jobs in New York. She began searching for career paths that were closely aligned to her passion and degree in Psychology. She loves working with teens. I guess you can say the apple doesn't fall to far from the tree! For those of you who may not know, the job market in Pennsylvania is more suitable for retired folk. The folk that just need to get out the house and shake their legs a little. Fast forward, my mom found a job at Covenant House in New York. Man oh, man was her approach different from my dad's.

Once my mom accepted her offer, she began to create a schedule. *What time did she need to get up to cook breakfast for her **grown** children? When should she wash clothes (and sometimes pack) my brothers' laundry for school and or practice? Is the fridge stocked enough with water and Gatorade, milk?* I had to ask her, "What is you doing baaaabbbeeee?" Everyone is grown. If they are hungry, they will either have a night of fasting and prayer, use their hands to make food, or buy it. Someone cannot find *their* t-shirt that *they* left carelessly in the living room and now *they* cannot find it... I guess they should have put *their* clothes where they were supposed to be. I did not want to sound like a Debbie Downer, but I wanted my mom to focus on herself. After all, she put her dreams and passions on hold to raise us. She did a damn good job might I add!

*   *   *   *   *

Clearly from the aforementioned scenarios, you can see the difference in priorities between man and woman. However, there are ways to treat yourself within the means of your obligations by using the 3 P's: **P**rioritize, **P**lan, and **P**roceed.

Prioritize: This step is essential because it gives you an opportunity to identify all the tasks that you currently have and allows you to assign a level of effort to each task. This way, you can focus on the most important task and defer the remaining tasks for another point

76

in time. Remember, we cannot have it all at the same time, but we sure as hell can work towards all of our goals at the same time.

Plan: Planning is key! We have all heard the saying before, "Fail to plan. Plan to fail." If we do not provide loose time frames and assess potential impacts to those time frames, we will never be able to reach our goals. I use the term "loose" time frame because it is easy for you to become overwhelmed or feel defeated because you did not complete one of twenty goals by December 23rd, 2019 at 8:05pm. Shit happens! Life happens! You *will* drop the ball sometimes. You will want to give up, but keep pushing!

As an illustration, you are saving for a house but you want to travel to Miami for a girls weekend because you want to *treat yourself.* Since you are saving to buy a house and *have* to travel to Miami, guess who needs to put themselves on a cash budget to avoid jeopardizing their savings account? That's right...YOU.

Another example— you may be a young mom and decide you are going out for a night on the town because you want to *treat yourself.* Well, guess what? Someone

78

needs to watch the baby. So here are your choices.

1) If you child attends daycare, you can take off of work and have a day date with yourself. You are now guaranteed a full eight hours without baby interruptions. You may not like the day vibe but get used to it because...well, you have obligations sis.

2) If you really cannot adapt to the day vibe as suggested in part one, then you can take off of work (let's say 1

Friday every month), get a baby sitter and DO YOU BOO!

See what I did there? Treat yourself... within the means of your obligations. You have to create a plan for your top priorities. Always remember, YOU are your first priority. You cannot pour from an empty vessel.

Proceed: The last and final step is to proceed. This is the step where you execute and enjoy. It is just that simple. Proceed with happiness, peace, joy, and of course a little bit of caution and a whole lot of resilience. Nevertheless, embrace

80

failures and enjoy the journey to a better you!

Using the 3P's is an iterative process. I repeat:

The journey to self-discovery is hard and uncomfortable, yet beautiful. You will have to regroup and reset, and start all over. Again and again times infinity. Just remember you deserve it *and* all of your goals coming to fruition too. Keep the 3P's in your head whenever you treat yourself.

Don't worry, you got this girl!

6

CHOOSE YOU...

EVERY
SINGLE
TIME

Now you know I could not share all of these tips without showing you how to retain the good vibes that you'll be attracting! Every tip that I have shared with you on how to woman up, boils down to one simple rule: Choose you— Every. Single. Damn. Time. Over and over and over again. And most importantly, don't you ever feel guilty for doing so.

I will admit that this rule is easier said than done. As women it is our nature to want to nurture. We want to be everything for everyone at all times. Most times we tend to feel guilty when we put our needs in front of others. There is a sense of estrangement because the idea of prioritizing our happiness feels selfish. Between the 3P's, acknowledging your accomplishments, knowing your ministry, remembering your value and being aware of the vibe you bring, you will be able to choose yourself. EVERY. SINGLE. TIME.

Choose yourself means prioritizing your health: mental, spiritual, physical, and emotional. Need a therapist—get one. Need motivation—surround yourself with people who are where you aspire to

Be or watch motivational Youtube videos for free 99. Need to drop 20, 30, 50 pounds—meal prep and get to working out, hire a personal trainer. Just choose yourself and work towards becoming a better version of you. Remember, you are here for a purpose and every day that you are breathing is another chance for you to get that much closer to your destiny.

*   *   *   *   *

When I first graduated from Hampton University with my MBA, I was so motivated to go back home and help my family both financially and academically. Long story short, I chose to over extend myself financially, mentally and spiritually which resulted in extreme weight gain and lack of motivation to do anything. In those three years I was home, I became stressed and overwhelmed because I hated my job and felt like no one understood what I was going through. I was the first one in my household to graduate college.

Being the oldest child, I was the first to experience life. I did not have an older sibling to learn from or to bounce ideas off of. I wanted to be the first person my brothers would look up to as a benchmark for milestones (i.e., going to school, buying a car, purchasing a home). This expectation that I placed on myself resulted in depression. It took me almost a year to find a therapist because I was not sure or I should say, I was not ready to *address* all dimensions of me. There were so many thoughts that ran through my mind:

How can strong a minded, confident Kysha be depressed? Me of all people. How can valedictorian of her high school class, MBA recipient, consultant of a Big

4

accounting firm be sitting here, in this predicament. Mentally, physically, emotionally and spiritually unhealthy. Unhappy. Unsatisfied. Unfulfilled.

I made it my priority to get back to Kysha; genuine, happy, spiritual Kysha. So, *I chose* to find a therapist even while I was crying. I solicited friends and family members to help me on my journey to seeking a therapist because my mind was no longer my own. It was through therapy that I learned how to set boundaries, repurpose my energy to situations and people that mattered, and began to seek internal validation. It was through therapy that I was reminded that *I was* worth the effort; that *I* was my greatest investment; that I got the JUICE; that I am *that* chick! I figured for once in my life that I should take the brilliant advice that I am always sharing. Although I am still going to therapy, I am glad that I took the initial jump to *address* all the dimensions of me.

If you are interested in some of the challenges that I experienced when searching for a therapist, you can listen to the *Lights Please Podcast Series* on any platform where you stream your podcasts. The episode about mental illness is called *I'm Going Crazy, Crazy, Crazy*.

My priority will always be me and anyone who cannot understand that, can be dismissed. I am still on the journey to self-discovery and one thing that I have learned is that I never want to lose me again; it cost too much. My aura is exclusive; you need a personal invitation to bask in my company and use my energy. Yes that may sound uppity or boujee , but hey...this is my life and I am in control of it! I will always choose me, EVERY

SINGLE DAMN TIME. ...and so should you!

CLOSING REMARKS

M y purpose in life is to educate and empower young women to tap into their superpower; to be a living example of what it means when you choose yourself EVERY SINGLE DAMN TIME! To show young girls that you can still be who you want to be, do what you want to do, and go where you want to go despite the detours on this ride called life.

Baby girl, you are the prize and you have a superpower that is beyond this world. It is *not* your ministry to convince people of your superpower. It is *not* your ministry to be everything for everyone at all times. It is *not* your ministry to try and do everything all at once to keep up with societal standards. However, it is *your* ministry to understand the power and vibe you bring to *any* setting. It is *your* ministry to always know your worth and remember your value. It is *your* ministry to praise yourself for just making it another day, taking another step, and being here in the moment. It is *your* ministry to treat yourself and choose you. EVERY. SINGLE. DAMN TIME.

ABOUT THE AUTHOR

Shackysha Renée is a Leadership and Lifestyle Coach. Her life mantra is 'the best is yet to come.' She believes there is always room for self- reflection and improvement. There are always more dreams to dream, more goals to accomplish, more love to give, more wisdom to impart on others. Shackysha has always been an advocate for self- empowerment, especially for women. She believes that women have a superpower that is beyond this world. Her passion for empowering women and mentoring was the driving force behind Woman Up Enterprise.

Woman Up Enterprise is a company that primarily teaches high school and college females how to own their superpower of being a woman while providing them tools that will help guide them to becoming the fearless, strong beings they were created to be!

Through speaking engagements, open forums, podcast series, and branded products, both women and men are able to show their support for the strong women in their lives. It is essential that women have a support system to connect and strive in a world that consistently overlooks and undermine their value.

STAY CONNECTED !

INSTAGRAM

@womanup.enterprise

@lights.ple4se

FACEBOOK

womanup.enterprise

TWITTER

@shackysha.renee

EMAIL

shackysharenee@womanupenterprise.com

Made in the USA
Lexington, KY
20 November 2019